C000274853

After All We've Done!

To Mum and Dad,

Happy Anniversary 1986

lots
of love
Emma x

FOR JACKIE , JON , SI , & BEN .

After All We've Done!

JOHN ASTROP

Patrick Hardy Books

PATRICK HARDY BOOKS
1 Newburgh Street,
London W1V 1LH, UK

Text & Illustrations Copyright ©1984 by John Astrop

All rights reserved. No part of this publication
may be reproduced, stored in a retrieval system,
or transmitted in any form or by any means,
electronic, mechanical, photocopying, recording,
or otherwise, without the prior permission of the
copyright owner.

First published in Great Britain 1984
by Patrick Hardy Books

ISBN 0 7444 0048 1

Printed in Great Britain

FOR JACKIE., JON, SI, & BEN.

'OF COURSE HE'S YOUR **REAL** FATHER!'

' YOU WERE MAD ABOUT THAT STUFF
EARLIER THIS EVENING !! '

WHY THE HELL CAN'T **YOU** BE A SUPERSTAR?

'IF YOU REALLY WANT TO KNOW DAD...
I'M EXPERIMENTING WITH A
DEADLY WEAPON!!'

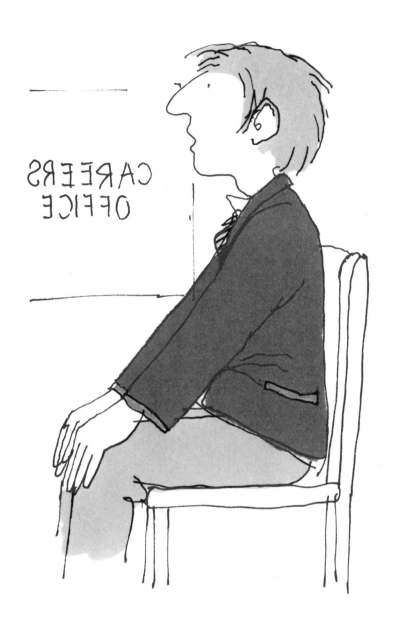

'...WELL, SIR - I THOUGHT I MIGHT GO IN
FOR WHEELING & DEALING, SIR ...
A LITTLE BIT HERE, SIR ... ,
A LITTLE BIT THERE ... '

'VERY FUNNY DAD - I'M LAUGHING
HA-HA - HA-HA ! '

'...WHY CAN'T YOU USE YOUR SPARE TIME
CONSTRUCTIVELY - THINK OF YOUR FUTURE,
GO AND PLAY **SNOOKER** OR **DARTS**!!'

' PLEASE DON'T FEEL **WE** ARE PUTTING ANY PRESSURE ON YOU DEAR – IF YOU WANT TO BE A PATHETIC FAILURE THAT'S UP TO YOU!

'ARE YOU KEEPING SOMETHING FROM US!'

'WHAT'S A SADO-MASOCHISTIC
TRANSEXUAL, MA?'

' WHAT DO YOU MEAN, YOU **KNOW** WHAT IT'S LIKE TO BE A FATHER ?'

'REVOLTING AND IMPOSSIBLE AS IT MAY SEEM - WE'RE LIVING EVIDENCE THAT THEY DID IT !! *UGH!!*'

'BE WITH YOU IN A MINUTE MUM...
... ONLY TWO MORE!'

'IN YOU GO BECKY. THEY WON'T SHRINK IN WATER, YOU KNOW!'

'WHAT HE'S DOING, MRS CRESSWELL IS
QUITE NATURAL...WORRYING, YES...
BUT QUITE NATURAL MRS CRESSWELL!'

'ANYBODY IN ?'

' SO **THIS** IS RICK ! ! '

'SO 'MEATLOAF' IS **MARRIED** - IT'S NOT THE END
OF THE WORLD, YOU KNOW!'

MA! COULD **I** HAVE THE MALE MENOPAUSE?
I FEEL EXTREMELY LETHARGIC!

'MISS CLARKE SAYS I'M ATTENTION SEEKING – WHAT MUST YOU **ALL** BE THINKING OF ME!'

.. WHY DON'T YOU TWO GO OFF AND PLAY
'INVADERS'!!'

'HELL! THE DAMN LOCUSTS HAVE STRIPPED
THE KITCHEN BARE AGAIN!... NOT ONE
BLOODY BISCUIT LEFT!'

'EXACTLY **HOW** OLD
IS THIS OLDER WOMAN DEAR!'

'DADDY AND I DON'T MIND, BUT COULD YOU LET IT DOWN WHEN GRAN COMES?'

'DAD - YOU NEVER GIVE ME EYE-CONTACT WHEN I ASK YOU ABOUT SEX !'

'COURSE I'M **UP** MA! JUST LOOKING FOR A CLEAN SHIRT!'

' YOU TREAT THIS PLACE LIKE A
'MACDONALDS' ! '

'THE ONE **IGNORING** ME POINTEDLY
IS MY SON.'

'WE **DO** UNDERSTAND YOU PHILIPPA —
WE JUST DON'T **LIKE** YOU, THAT'S ALL!'

'NICE THOUGHT DAD, BUT I WENT ON IT
TWO YEARS AGO ! '

'B.O.! MALCOLM!'

'WHAT D'YOU MEAN 'VOW OF CELIBACY'?
WE THOUGHT YOU **WERE**!'

' ANYONE SEEN THE LAST TIN OF CATFOOD?
THERE'S ONLY A CAN OF SPAGHETTI
SAUCE IN HERE ! '

'LET'S DO SOMETHING REALLY **WILD** WITH YOURS, MUM!'

'BARRY! YOUR ROOM'S IMMACULATE
AGAIN — WHAT'S GOING ON UP THERE!!'

'OK! GO FOR COMPUTER STUDIES, BUT KEEP UP
THE SNOOKER. THEN YOU'VE ALWAYS GOT
SOMETHING STEADY TO FALL BACK ON!'

'ALRIGHT - **WHO** HID THE BARRY MANILOW ?'

'OH **GOD**! KEV'S BEEN MAKING ANGEL DELIGHT AGAIN!!'

'MUM - **GUESS** WHO'S PREGNANT!'

'COULD MY **LITTLE GIRL** LEND HER OL' DAD
A QUID 'TIL THE END OF THE WEEK?'

...**KATY**...DO WE KNOW A 'LOVERLIPS'?!'

'...HEAR ALL ...SEE ALL ... AND SAY NOWT

'...I CAN'T **BELIEVE** I'M HEARING THIS FROM **OUR** LITTLE EMILY!'

' IT'S 'BOIL IN THE BAG' FROM NOW ON DAD...
I'M JOINING MUM AT GREENHAM ! '

'YOU'RE OVER-REACTING DEBBIE –
NOBODY'S GOING TO NOTICE
ONE LITTLE SPOT!'

'I'VE TRIED...GOD KNOWS I'VE TRIED...
BUT I KEEP COMING BACK TO THE
CHILDREN'S BLOODYMINDEDNESS !'

'DON'T ASK ME CYNTH, **I** ONLY LENT YOU THE SLEEPING BAG . . . '

'MASSES OF MODELS ARE ADVERTISING HERE
MAYBE I SHOULD . . .'

'I SAID YOUR FATHER AND I ARE DECORATING...NOT SEPARATING!'

'PERHAPS · **EGON** · YOU'LL GIVE US YOUR
GASTRONOMIC CRITIQUE OF THE SUBTLE,
NUANCES OF THE 'ESTOUFFADE DE BOEUF'!

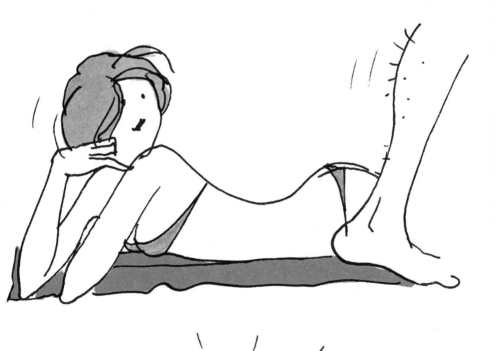

'LET'S FACE IT DEAR . . . 'JOLLY HOCKEY-STICKS' ARE **OVER** ! ! '

'OH MUM ! NOT THE PHOTOS...**PLEASE** !

'I THINK WE CAN SAFELY SAY THAT ALL IDEAS OF JULIAN BECOMING A BRAIN SURGEON ARE KNOCKED ON THE HEAD!'

'**WE DO**, WE **DO**, LIKE POP - WE JUST LIKE
IT MUCH, MUCH, QUIETER !!'

'FRAID THE FAMILY HOLIDAY'S OFF THIS YEAR
— YOU'LL HAVE TO GO WITH A FRIEND!'

'AN 'A' LEVEL IN TECHNICAL DRAWING
IS NOT GOING TO SAVE YOU!!.'

'ONLY NUMBER THREE!-SURE YOU'RE
NOT GETTING ANOREXIA?'

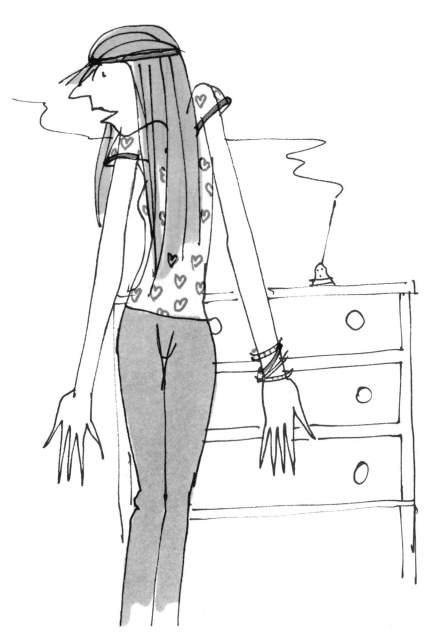

'MUM – I DON'T NEED DRUG REHABILITATION –
IT'S ONLY A JOSS STICK!'

' DID YOU FIND THE 'MONOPOLY', KIDS!

' YOU'RE JUST NOT GIVING YOURSELF A
CHANCE SON, WITH HAIR LIKE THAT ! '

'...IT WORRIES ME...YOU ALWAYS SEEM TO HAVE **ENOUGH** MONEY!!'

'WHAT THE **HELL** ARE YOU DOING ! ! ! '

'...AND I'M NOT **TOUCHING** YOUR ROOM 'TIL YO
REMOVE THE DEAD SOCKS!'

'...AND ARE YOUR PANTS CLEAN ?...
I'D FEEL **TERRIBLE** IF YOU WERE
KNOCKED DOWN & RUN OVER
WITH DIRTY PANTS !'

' STOP IT GEORGE ! SHE COULD BE
IN THE OTHER ROOM ! '

'..AND ANOTHER THING – YOUR MOTHER WAS
NEVER HOME BEFORE MIDNIGHT – AND SHE...'

'YOU'RE **NOT** CREEPING OFF
WITH MY DEMIS ROUSSOS
ALBUMS, ARE YOU?'

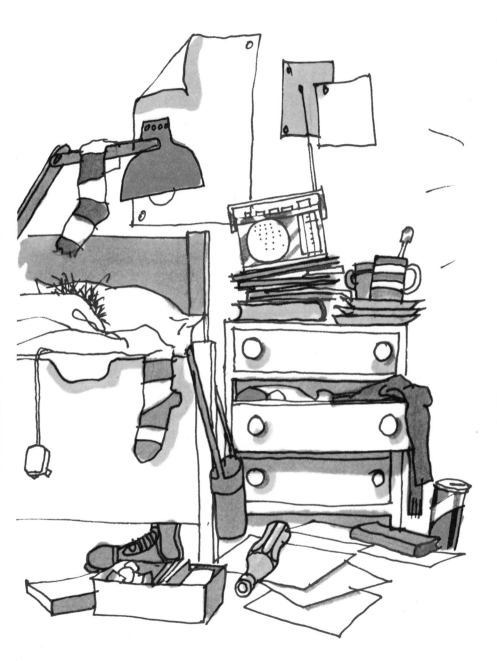

'IS THAT **YOU** IN THERE, OR HAVE YOU ACQUIRED A STUFFED HEDGHOG!'

'ANY CHANCE OF YOU DOING A CLEAN-UP JOB ON GALACTIC HEADQUARTERS!?'

'KEEP UP WITH US GLORIA AND TAKE
NO NOTICE OF THEM !'

' THE WORLD ENDS IN PRECISELY
TWO AND A HALF SECOND'S TIME !'

IT'S **YOUR** MONEY, IT'S **YOUR** BUSINESS,
IF YOU WANT TO MAKE AN EMBARRASSING
SPECTACLE OF YOURSELF... DON'T ASK **ME**!'

'ANYONE SEEN THE CORNED BEEF
FOR TONIGHT'S SUPPER ?

IF THAT BLOODY BOY HAS SKOFFED IT..

'...WELL IF YOU'RE NOT GOING TO HAVE A BATH, DO YOU MIND IF I **DUST** YOU?'

'OH THAT'S NOTHING - MINE'S GOT A MOHICAN, BOTH EARS PIERCED TWICE, , GREEN HAIR, **AND** A NOSE-PIN ! '

'YOUR FATHER AND I ARE **NOT** THE BEST
PEOPLE TO ASK ABOUT SEX ...
... AT THE MOMENT !!'

WHAT WOULD YOU THINK IF YOUR **FATHER**
CAME HOME WEARING AN EAR-RING ?'

'NO MUM! I'M NOT PUTTING THAT AWFUL
GREEN STUFF ON MY HAIR!'

'...AND WHY CAN'T YOU HAVE NICE **LONG** HAI?
LIKE EVERYONE ELSE?'

OF COURSE I UNDERSTAND EQUAL RIGHTS...
I JUST DON'T SEE YOU AS A LUMBERJACK!'

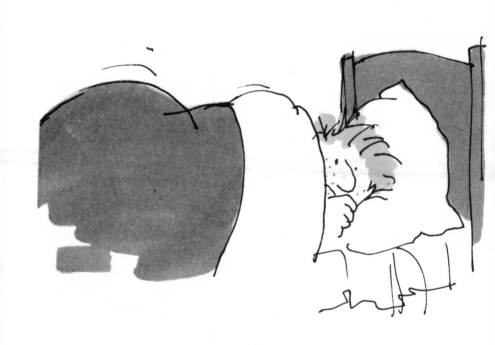

' ACNE HAS **NEVER** BEEN TERMINAL DENNIS

'S'O·K GRAN, S'ME, TONY!!'

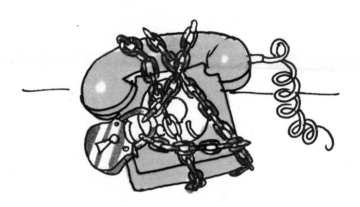